IL: MG BL4.0 AR0.5points

Deadly Predators

By Louise and
Richard Spilsbury

Jump into the cockpit and
take flight with Pilot books.
Your journey will take you on
high-energy adventures as you
learn about all that is wild,
weird, fascinating, and fun!

This edition first published in 2017 by Bellwether Media, Inc.

No part of this publication may be reproduced in whole or in part without written permission of the publisher.
For information regarding permission, write to Bellwether Media, Inc., Attention: Permissions Department,
5357 Penn Avenue South, Minneapolis, MN 55419.

Library of Congress Cataloging-in-Publication Data

Names: Spilsbury, Louise, author. | Spilsbury, Richard, 1963- author.
Title: Deadly Predators / by Louise and Richard Spilsbury.
Other titles: Pilot (Bellwether Media)
Description: Minneapolis, MN : Bellwether Media, Inc., 2017. | Series: Pilot.
  Engineered by Nature | Audience: Ages 7-13. | Audience: Grades 3 to
  8. | Includes bibliographical references and index.
Identifiers: LCCN 2016033340 (print) | LCCN 2016036288 (ebook) | ISBN
  9781626175891 (hardcover : alk. paper) | ISBN 9781681033198 (ebook)
Subjects: LCSH: Predatory animals–Juvenile literature. | Predation
  (Biology)–Juvenile literature. | Animal behavior–Juvenile literature.
Classification: LCC QL758 .S65 2017 (print) | LCC QL758 (ebook) | DDC
  591.5/3–dc23
LC record available at https://lccn.loc.gov/2016033340

Printed in the United States of America, North Mankato, MN.

Table of Contents

Catch and Kill!

Animals are **engineered** by nature to survive in their **habitats**. Some have **adaptations**, or features, that make them deadly **predators**. Predators are animals that catch and kill other animals to eat.

Predators are found on land, in water, and in the sky. Some land predators have strong legs and sharp teeth. These help them chase down and kill **prey**. Predators in the air are adapted to attack from above. Predators in the water may sting, bite, or even give victims an **electric shock**!

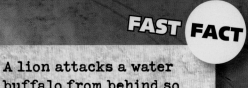

A lion attacks a water buffalo from behind so it does not get stabbed by its prey's sharp horns!

DID YOU KNOW?

A lion's powerful jaws trap prey and deliver a deadly bite. These fierce predators can catch and kill animals much bigger than themselves.

Boa Constrictor

A boa constrictor lies in wait at night. It keeps very still. It can smell prey when it is near. It can also sense the body heat that animals give off.

When an animal passes by, the boa strikes. The snake's mouth is lined with sharp teeth that curve backward. They tightly grasp and hold the prey.

DID YOU KNOW?

A boa grips its victim so tight that blood and oxygen cannot reach the animal's organs. The victim can die within seconds.

A boa does not hunt every day. Its body takes four to six days to break down food.

The boa winds its long body around its prey. It slowly squeezes the animal to death. With its mouth wide open, it starts to swallow its victim whole!

Polar Bear

A polar bear can smell a bearded seal from almost a mile away. When it spots the seal, it starts to crawl toward its prey.

If the seal looks around, the polar bear freezes! It keeps very still. The seal cannot see it. The bear's white coloring provides **camouflage** against the snow and ice.

FAST FACT

A polar bear's claws are curved to catch and trap prey. They also help the bear grip the slippery ice.

bearded seal

When the bear is close, it charges! It runs and grabs the seal in its claws or teeth. There is no escape!

Cheetah

A cheetah **stalks** a young gazelle across the grassland. It moves slowly through the tall grass. It silently sneaks up close to its prey.

DID YOU KNOW?

A cheetah is the fastest land animal in the world. It can run 328 feet (100 meters) in just 5.95 seconds.

Suddenly, the cheetah sprints toward the gazelle. The gazelle runs fast, too. The cheetah's powerful legs take huge strides. Its long tail helps it balance when it changes direction at high speed. The cheetah makes a final dash. Its sharp teeth sink into the gazelle's neck. The chase is over.

FAST FACT

A cheetah's paws have claws that dig into the ground. The paws also have grooves that grip the ground.

ACTIVITY

Engineering in Practice

The cheetah's paws are designed to grip. This helps it run fast. Are your shoes engineered to grip, too?

- Find some shoes with different soles. Choose some that are smooth, shiny, rough, grooved, and spiked like soccer cleats.
- Take the shoes outside. Rub each sole one way over a dirt or gravel path.
- What do you notice? Which sole grips best? Why do you think that is?

King Cobra

The deadly king cobra mainly feeds on other snakes. It hides and lies patiently in wait for a victim. When it is ready to strike, the snake raises its head.

Suddenly, the cobra darts down. It sinks its sharp, hollow **fangs** into its victim. Like needles, these teeth inject deadly **venom** into the prey.

FAST FACT

A king cobra flicks out its tongue to pick up the scent of its prey.

The venom in the cobra's bite **paralyzes** and kills the victim. Then the snake opens its jaws wide and swallows its supper whole.

Crocodile

A crocodile does not normally chase prey. It hides in the water and waits. Its eyes, ears, and nose are on the top of its head. If its body is underwater, it can still see, hear, and breathe.

When an animal comes to drink, the crocodile strikes! It uses its tail and strong back legs to spring quickly out of the water. It seizes its victim in its powerful mouth. Its jaws can snap bones like twigs!

Box Jellyfish

The box jellyfish swims along. Long **tentacles** hang from its body. These tentacles can be 10 feet (3 meters) long. Each tentacle is covered in about 5,000 tiny darts. Each dart is loaded with powerful venom!

When the tentacles brush against a fish or shrimp, they release a dart. The painful venom **stuns** prey. This keeps it from damaging the jellyfish's delicate tentacles. The jellyfish moves its prey toward its mouth, then feasts.

tentacles

ACTIVITY

Engineering in Practice

Try this cool activity to see how a
jellyfish moves!

- Blow up a balloon, then pinch the
  end closed so no air escapes.
- Now, let it go!
- The balloon should move quickly
  forward, as the air is pushed out
  of it. This is similar to the way a
  jellyfish uses jets of water to move.

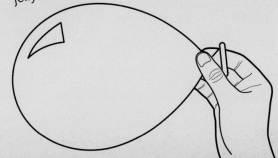

Great White Shark

A great white shark swims slowly in the ocean. When it spots a sea lion, it quickly shoots up through the water! The shark's body is **streamlined**. It is long and thin. This helps it move through the water like an arrow. As it leaps from the water, the shark opens its mouth.

DID YOU KNOW?

Great white sharks have an excellent sense of smell. They can smell small amounts of blood from more than 3 miles (5 kilometers) away.

It grabs its prey tightly in several rows of sharp, jagged teeth. Then it crushes, chomps, and swallows its victim underwater.

FAST FACT

A great white shark has about 300 teeth. If it loses a tooth, another one is ready to replace it.

Electric Eel

The electric eel lives in muddy pools and rivers. It has poor eyesight. To hunt, it sends out a small **electrical** signal. It uses this like **radar** to find prey.

The electric eel has parts inside its body that store electrical power. It is like the eel has its own batteries! When a fish comes near, the eel releases a burst of electricity. This stuns the fish.

Then the electric eel sucks its prey into its mouth and straight into its stomach!

DID YOU KNOW?

Some electric eels are huge. They can grow to more than 8 feet (2.5 meters) long.

Harpy Eagle

A harpy eagle waits in a high rain forest tree. It sits there for hours. When it spots a monkey, it takes flight.

The eagle quickly swoops in for the kill. When it is close to its prey, it stretches out its huge **talons**. It grasps the monkey in these strong claws.

The eagle carries its victim to a high branch. It uses its powerful feet to crush and kill its prey. Then it uses its sharp, hooked beak to feast.

FAST FACT

A harpy eagle's wings measure 6.5 feet (2 meters) across.

The harpy eagle's deadly talons are 5 inches (13 centimeters) long. That's as long as a grizzly bear's claws!

Great Horned Owl

The great horned owl usually hunts at night. It sits on a branch, listening for prey. It twists its head so it can see all around. When it spots a victim, it silently takes off.

DID YOU KNOW?

Huge eyes help owls hunt for prey in low light. If a great horned owl was as big as a human, its eyes would be the size of oranges!

A great horned owl eats its prey whole. It then spits up bones and other parts its body cannot break down.

Its wide wings have a fringe of feathers. These soft feathers reduce the sound of air rushing through them. Prey cannot hear the owl approaching! It grabs its prey in its wide talons and flies off to feed.

Vampire Bat

At night, a vampire bat leaves its cave. While it flies, it sends out sounds. The sounds **echo** back, signaling to the bat where to find a victim.

The bat lands and crawls onto a sleeping cow. The bat's nose senses hot blood flowing under the cow's skin.

The bat sinks its thin, sharp teeth into its victim. It then laps up the blood with its tongue. The bat's **saliva** keeps the blood from **clotting** while it drinks.

FAST FACT

To survive, a vampire bat must hunt every one to two days.

ACTIVITY

Engineering in Practice

To see how sound reflects off an object, try making an echo yourself.

- Stand a long distance from a wall.
- Clap loudly.
- Listen for the echo. The distance it travels is twice the distance from you to the wall (because the sound has to travel to the wall and back).

Engineered to Survive

Adaptations help animals survive. On land, a polar bear's white coloring helps it sneak up on seals. A cheetah's long, strong legs help it chase fast gazelles.

In water, a box jellyfish's tentacles help it catch prey. A crocodile's teeth keep large prey from escaping. In the air, an owl's silent flight and an eagle's strong talons help them catch food. Without these features, these animals could not get the food they need to survive!

FAST FACT

If an octopus loses an arm, it grows a new one to replace it!

sucker

DID YOU KNOW?

An octopus has eight arms covered in suckers. It uses its suckers to grip its prey. The octopus then injects venom into its victim.

Glossary

adaptations—features or characteristics that an organism has that help it survive

camouflage—colors or patterns that help an animal blend in with its surroundings

clotting—becoming thick and sticky to stop blood from flowing

echo—to bounce a sound back

electric shock—an injury caused when electricity passes through an animal's body

electrical—producing a form of energy called electricity

engineered—designed and built

fangs—long, sharp teeth

habitats—the natural areas in which organisms live

paralyzes—keeps an animal from moving

predators—animals that catch and eat other animals

prey—animals that are eaten by other animals

radar—a device that sends out radio waves to find out where an object is

saliva—spit

stalks—hunts slowly and silently

streamlined—having a narrow, smooth shape that moves quickly through air and water

stuns—confuses an animal's senses, usually by a blow

talons—long, sharp claws

tentacles—long, flexible arms

venom—poison produced by some animals

To Learn More

AT THE LIBRARY

Burnie, David, Miranda Smith, and Claire Llewellyn. *Deadly Creatures: A Thrilling Adventure with Nature's Fiercest Hunters*. New York, N.Y.: Kingfisher, 2016.

Claybourne, Anna. *Scanorama: Deadly Predators*. San Diego, Calif.: Silver Dolphin Books, 2016.

Stewart, Melissa. *National Geographic Readers: Deadly Predators*. Washington, D.C.: National Geographic Children's Books, 2013.

ON THE WEB

Learning more about deadly predators is as easy as 1, 2, 3.

1. Go to www.factsurfer.com.
2. Enter "deadly predators" into the search box.
3. Click the "Surf" button and you will see a list of related websites.

With factsurfer.com, finding more information is just a click away.

Index

The images in this book are reproduced through the courtesy of: Sergey Uryadnikov/ Shutterstock, front cover, pp. 1, 8–9, 14–15; Alta Oosthuizen/ Shutterstock, pp. 4–5; James Gerholdt/ Getty Images, pp. 6–7; Prosicky/ Shutterstock, p. 9 (middle); Stuart G Porter/ Shutterstock, pp. 10–11; CraigBurrows/ Shutterstock, pp. 12–13; Enrique Ramos/ WorldFoto/ Alamy Stock Photo, pp. 16–17; Martin Prochazkacz/ Shutterstock, pp. 18–19; WaterFrame/ Alamy Stock Photo, pp. 20–21; Nick Garbutt/ Nature Picture Library / Alamy Stock Photo, pp. 22–23; MarcusVDT/ Shutterstock, p. 23 (top); Mlorenz/ Shutterstock, pp. 24–25; Michael Lynch/ Shutterstock, pp. 26–27; Olga Visavi/ Shutterstock, pp. 28–29.